D1577203

DOLCE & GABBANA

Translated from the French by Marguerite Shore

First published in Great Britain in 1999
by Thames and Hudson Ltd, London

Copyright © 1998 Éditions Assouline, Paris

British Library Cataloguing-in-Publication Data
A catalogue record for this book is available from the British Library

ISBN 0-500-01921-5

Printed and bound in Italy

DOLCE & GABBANA

Franca Sozzani

Thames and Hudson

a play of black fabric draped around the body enhances the female form. The models have defined, sensual, rounded shapes, their breasts supported by black bras, their waists and hips restrained within close-fitting corsets. Sultry girls with dark eyes evoke the women of the South: carnal and provocative, yet austere and haughty.

It is the woman of the South. It is Sicily, native land of Domenico Dolce, that is the inspiration behind the Dolce & Gabbana line. It is the mystery of a place where everything is interwoven. The stereotype of the Sicilian that lives on in the common imagination—a man dressed in black, wearing a white shirt and peasant's cap, and who, on the hottest of days, roams the cactus fields and orange groves, wearing only a white tank top—is interwoven with the figures of women, so beloved by Sciascia, described as enveloped within their black shawls, traversing the countryside, hiding themselves from the eyes of others.

Dolce and Gabbana have appropriated these images from Italian culture and traditional Sicilian literature. Their clothing is imbued with a narrative power, suggested by their own cherished land, emphasized by the pride of those who know it well. But their inspiration doesn't stop with the land, which is only their history, their past—for they are looking forward, toward the future.

"We cannot limit ourselves to a single style, it's not natural, no one wants to be always and only the same," says Stefano Gabbana. According to Domenico Dolce, "Fashion today is fifty percent attitude, and what makes you feel sexy, modern, or old, interesting, or squalid is only attitude."

"The Dolce & Gabbana woman is inspired by the realism of Verga's novels and by the atmosphere of realist cinema. It is mysterious, self-possessed, feminine." (Antonella Amapane, *La Stampa*)

The designers interweave the way Sicilian peasants dress with the way actors in films by Rossellini, Pasolini or Visconti dress. "Now that Fellini, Rossellini, Pasolini, Visconti are gone, all we have is Dolce & Gabbana, neorealist fashion!" says Madonna. Cinema is an integral part of their history, and when they are designing, they think about the film's direction, the characters, the costumes, and the decor. Their images are drawn from women ranging from Silvana Mangano to Anna Magnani. Dolce & Gabbana's woman is sexy, shapely, strong, and Mediterranean; three contemporary icons— Isabella Rossellini, Linda Evangelista, and Madonna—represent her. The designers favor women with strong personalities, women who are proud of their bodies.

Dolce and Gabbana turn women into stars; make them feel like true divas. "The first piece of theirs that I wore was a white shirt, cut in such a way that my breasts appeared to be exploding." (Isabella Rossellini)

"They made a clean sweep of all the aesthetics that dominated the 1980s and now, in another direction, in their escapes, voyages against the tide, ethereal dreams." (Gianluca Lo Vetro, *L'Unità*)

They love to provoke and to scandalize. "They are so exuberant, politically incorrect! And so fresh." (Patrick McCarthy, *WWD*)

5

dolce & Gabbana don't obey the rules, every season is a surprise; they mix the baroque with plastic, crochet with Velcro, brocade with mirrors. They can evoke images of decorum and Sicilian aristocracy or create an emblematic worker in a tank top; they can surprise us with their new Ophelias or subvert the sexiness of a garment with animal spots. They play with *La Dolce Vita*, with paparazzi and divas to evoke a world of amusement, a world of nights spent on the Via Veneto in search of a famous director. They use furs, low-cut dresses, and fake diamonds (1990). It is ironic, it is theater, and it is unexpected. And they shoot new scenes with the same spontaneity. The China Collection (1992) is full of embroidery, dragons, colors, just as The Leopard Collection (1988) synthesized the Sicilian aristocratic and peasant worlds with an explosion of velvets, ball gowns, ruffled shirt fronts, women in men's suits with vests, white shirts, peasant caps. In October 1992, the passage to "hippie-chic"—with flowered dresses, platform shoes, Marianne Faithfull make-up and trousers with a Carnaby Street silhouette—was full of fantasy, a search for fabrics such as patchwork, brocades and embroidery, and mixtures of pin-stripes and lace. This was the collection that led Suzy Menkes (*The International Herald Tribune*) to say that Dolce and Gabbana have the ability to mix periods and countries, male and female wardrobes, Swinging London and Biedermeier period, and they do so in a way that it all becomes Dolce & Gabbana. "It worked," she wrote in March of 1993. So much so that even *WWD* wrote, that same year, "They are the darlings of the moment."

Sicily, folk, the 1800s, hippies: quotations from the past are present in their designs without their being retro. There is always an air of today, a curiosity about new directions—it is not *divertissement* as an end in itself. Thus, in 1994, Dolce & Gabbana took a new direction: they abandoned the 1970s look as well as corsets and bras, and their new woman emerged—more along the aesthetic lines of K. D. Lang than those of a pinup. Isabella Rossellini is a prime example of this "Sapphic-chic" masculine style, and Dolce & Gabbana's models that are dressed in this style— with men's clothing and slicked-down hair—look less like provocative sex symbols than Mafioso bosses from the 1930s or neorealist actors in T-shirts, such as Massimo Girotti. "The collection was boyishly androgynous. It worked perfectly on all the girls. . . ." (Alison Veness, *The Independent*)

That same year the two designers moved from the runway to the movie set, appearing in Tornatore's film, *L'Uomo delle Stelle* (*The Starmaker*). Tornatore also created their sensual, erotically-charged perfume TV commercial with Monica Bellucci, set in their beloved Sicily. Dolce and Gabbana's love of strong images lead them to choose the most talented photographers to produce their advertising campaigns.

"They bring together the most disparate evocations. Corsets and petit-point, the homeless and a frescoed universe, but the one constant in their work is the South. The Mediterranean prevails as a leitmotif. Their meeting with photographer Ferdinando Scianna [who until that time had not been involved with fashion] proved to be fateful and led to a successful series of images, full of humor and a southern flavor." (Renata Molho, *Il Sole 24 Ore*)

Steven Meisel continues to create Dolce & Gabbana ad

campaigns using female icons ranging from Bellucci, who revives Fellini's *La Dolce Vita;* to Linda Evangelista, who depicts the stance and clothing of the women of the South; to the extremely modern 1998 campaign, which leaves behind all suggestions and evocations and presents a "clear" interpretation of fashion, created with a light-box.

In 1995 they experienced a double conversion: first, in the winter collection, the Dolce & Gabbana woman played at being a well-bred lady, which, only the season before, would have provoked a horrified response—it quickly became "fashion's latest look." (Suzy Menkes, *The International Herald Tribune*)

"These talented young men know where history is going and have shown things that, until recently, would have horrified us with their old-fashioned air, their refined style—well-dressed high fashion: little suits with the sleeves cut beneath the elbow which might have been worn by Sylva Koscina in *I Giovani Mariti (The Young Husbands,*1958); little coats with big, reassuring collars which might not have met with the approval of even Franca Valeri in *Parigi O Cara (Oh Dear, Paris,* 1962); sleek, long hair styles, flipped up at the ends like Catherine Spaak's in *La Voglia Matta (Crazy Desire)* (1962)." (Natalia Aspesi, *La Repubblica*)

Dolce and Gabbana were on the straight and narrow, declaring war on vulgarity as they moved into the next season. "After a holiday trip to the Aeolian Islands, they experienced a sort of 'conversion,' and the designers, who accustomed us to corsets and extremely provocative fashions, produced an extremely simple, clean, subtly sexy collection. The style is 'inspired without being gaudy' and is interpreted by Linda Evangelista as a version of the 'island' woman who, on the runway, never forgets to wear a rosary at her neck and a scarf on her head." (Laura Asnaghi, *La Repubblica*)

In the men's collection, too, there was the same irony and ability to play down the old classic "well-bred, respectable" gentleman. "Mr. Regular's entire wardrobe is brought up to date and made newly desirable." (Suzy Menkes, *The International Herald Tribune*)

t he play of colors and fabrics made these clothes modern. In 1996, Dolce & Gabbana's tenth anniversary, their first book was published. "The collection was simultaneously amusing, feminine, and sexy; a triumphant mix of Hollywood glamour. Models, with Grace Kelly chignons, wore '50s-style coats with large, printed roses and leopard-skin pants as well as the inevitable corsets." (Susannah Frankel, *The Guardian*)

The previous year had already been a triumph of leopard and animal prints for clothing, coats, and accessories. They had already used these animal prints on numerous occasions in earlier collections and immediately included them in the men's collections as well. Along with patchwork, animal prints became an identifying element of their style.

The designers covered the walls of their space (an old villa in the heart of Milan, surrounded by a large garden) with leopard and zebra-print fabric. The chairs, embellished with large "gilded curls," are covered with animal spots, as are the footstools and sofas.

In 1997 Dolce & Gabbana published a second "wild" book that included photos of their most important designs with animal prints, emphasizing that this was a characteristic of theirs that would make you claim this style as, "Mine!" (Suzy Menkes, *The International Herald Tribune*)

It was the same with the tank top! And in fact, they concluded their 1996 men's fashion show with a complete homage to Sicily, with young men in tank tops and pin-striped trousers, wearing leather slippers. The newspapers applauded, "Of course! It's southern Italian style."

b ut the duo continually evolves. They never stop searching. "They have demonstrated that they have matured, that they do not stay attached just to corsets and animal prints but have moved ahead, adding a feminine sweetness and new refinement to their decor and their details," Suzy Menkes (*The International Herald Tribune*) wrote in October of 1997. And it was in 1997 that they showed the cassock dress as a "must."

"Seven hundred meters of cardinal's cloth and *prie-dieu* cushions spiritually prepared the public for the 'priest' of designers. Here then is the 'mon-signora,' severe as a priest and more sumptuous than a cardinal." (Gianluca Lo Vetro, *L'Unità*)

With great lightness—in the presence of Demi Moore, a fan who exclaims, "I adore their lightness and simplicity"—the models file past, climbing down the steps: women covered in veils and butterflies, with hand-painted sacred-profane images of the Virgin Mary; tops worn with pants that stop below the knee; and undershirts covered with transparent black veils. Sacred hearts and small holy medals dangle as earrings. "This collection was fabulous, without question one of their most beautiful." (*WWD*)

Just when we thought the religious look was a "must" we could never do without, in March of 1998 the religious Sicilian in black was transformed into a romantic "cyber-Sicilian." (Laura Asnaghi, *La Repubblica*) Under a tent transformed into a Sicilian garden, "They offered a lesson on how to make brocades romantic, how to cut velvets, and how to transform pieces of the past—all with the help of modern technology. They dressed their models in stretch skirts of wool beneath tulle painted with flowers or in kimono-style silk coats decorated with mimosa—Palermo's botanical gardens inspired the hand-crafted flower designs. The collection consisted almost entirely of stretch fabric, with black, tailored coats and hem lines above the knee, made out of "mirror-effect" and elasticized plastic materials, with a sexy effect. It is the mix of softness and modern technology, combined with a delicate and traditional craftsmanship that gave their show its edge." (Suzy Menkes, *The International Herald Tribune*)

Modernity and the capacity to make everything current is what defines the Dolce & Gabbana style. "We want to use the past, but to project it into the future," say Domenico Dolce and Stefano Gabbana, leading us to understand that their quest has just begun.

DOLCE & GABBANA

Biography. Dolce & Gabbana Fashion Designers. Domenico Dolce (1958) was born in Polizzi Generosa (Palermo). From the time he was a young boy, he showed an interest in his father Saverio's small clothing business in Sicily. Stefano Gabbana (1962) was born in Milan, where he first studied graphics, then chose fashion as his true vocation. They worked together for several years in other designers' studios then went out on their own, establishing Dolce & Gabbana. They had their first independent fashion show in 1985, in Milan, where they exhibited their work under the New Talent category.

They immediately became the darlings of the press, and their ascent has continued as they establish new labels. Today they design a men's line, D&G, jeans, a bridal line, and knitwear. They have licenses for eye-wear, underwear, handbags, and shoes.

They have two perfumes, *Dolce & Gabbana* and *By Dolce & Gabbana*, and they are coming out with a complete line of cosmetics.

Their strength lies in their attention to Mediterranean culture, particularly the tradition of the South, thereby defining an unmistakable style.

Dolce & Gabbana Glossary

ANIMAL PRINT. Spotted or speckled pattern—reproduces the appearance of wild animals such as cheetahs, leopards, zebras, or panthers, or domestic animals such as the horse. It has been used by Dolce & Gabbana in great abundance, not only on leather but on fabrics and synthetic materials. Certainly it is one of the fundamental elements of their style, and it demonstrates how they have managed to couple the cultural tradition of the Baroque with eccentric and "wild" interventions.

BAROQUE, noun and adjective. A term that, on a cultural level, designates the historical period following the Counter-reformation in Catholic countries, characterized by art dense with virtuosic technique and flashiness, deliberately breaking away from Renaissance canons. The principal characteristics of the Baroque are the choice of plastic, animated forms, and a predilection for curving lines. In southern Italy, Naples was the main center for the dissemination of the Baroque. There were also significant Baroque achievements in Sicily, Palermo, and Catania and Noto.

In terms of Dolce & Gabbana's style, the term "baroque" has connotations of superabundance. This historical period has been a source for both their contributions to fashion and for the furnishings of their living and working spaces. Their houses, work spaces, and shops are decorated with grand curtains of red velvet, gilded frames, mirrors, and candelabra.

BLACK. Color; generally dark; sometimes qualitative by definition or correlation. Symbol of desperation, hostility. Favored by Visconti as a color of elegance: "Black, the color par excellence of beauty."

Black was adopted for Dolce & Gabbana's collections, for it is the basic color for the women and men of Sicily. It represents an entire culture and way of being.

BRA. noun. an elastic band with two cups to support and emphasize the female bosom. Female undergarment, the first examples of which date back to the early twentieth century. Until the mid-1920s, bras did not have underwires and were shaped to flatten the bosom and push it down.

In the 1940s the use of rubber padding gave additional shape to this garment, and in the 1950s its lines were exaggerated through the use of circular stitching that stiffened the fabric. During those years the strapless version became popular, to be worn under off-the-shoulder and low-cut dresses.

It is the most widely quoted Dolce & Gabbana fashion element. It is always shown and flaunted. The bra glimpsed beneath a cardigan or peeking out from a dress, usually in a contrasting color and fabric, has become a classic look.

BRASSIERE. In medieval times, a short, sleeveless undergarment. Worn by both sexes as a night dress, from the fourteenth to seventeenth centuries. Edged in fur, it was also used in winter. from those times until the twentieth century, the female bust has always been supported by reinforced corsets.

A fundamental element to Dolce & Gabbana's style, they have used it since their first collection, in 1985. Since then its use has been applied to every type of fabric, material, and embroidery. (see corset)

BROCADE. A fabric woven with a raised ornamental design. It can be richly decorated, and gold and silver threads are often used to form its designs. It is produced in various weights. Dolce & Gabbana uses silk or wool brocade for coats, vests, trousers and jackets and often lines them with speckled silk. Recently used for patchwork carpets and coverlets.

BUSTIER. Originating in the early nineteenth century, an undergarment that takes various forms. Was a short garment, with an emphasized waist, based on the model of a bra joined to a tank top that covers the back and pelvis. Shoulder-pads were placed far to the side, so they could be worn with boat-neck designs.

Used in the classical sense by Dolce & Gabbana, it has gradually been transformed into an outer garment or, made from cloth, into shirts.

CAMEO. A semi-precious stone, usually agate or onyx, on which a drawing is etched in relief. Very fashionable in the nineteenth century, it was pinned to a ribbon that was worn around the throat. Used a great deal in their early work, cameos have been used by Dolce & Gabbana to adorn purses, shoes, vests, and jackets, as well as for necklaces, buttons, and bracelets.

CORSAGE. A small bouquet of flowers pinned to the shoulder or breast. It can also become the border of a corselet in evening dresses. Traditionally, violets, gardenias, and camellias were most often used. This accessory often appears in the Dolce & Gabbana collections, both to emphasize the neckline of dresses and corselets, as well as to ornament jackets and purses. The flowers vary according to the season and style. The latest corsage was made from mimosa, for the winter 1998 collection.

CORSELET. An undergarment popular until the 1920s. Based on a tank top, it had many ribs, was padded, and fastened with ribbons to give the bust a rounded and curved line. The same length, or slightly longer, than the bust and extending down to the waist, it was later replaced by the bra.

It remains in its original version in the designers' collections, although modernized in proportions and bulk, and raised to the level of a real article of clothing in a woman's wardrobe. Fabrics used are always rich and unusual such as velvet, chiffon, satin, brocades, and, most recently, cellophane and lacquer.

CORSET, noun. A woman's corselet, elastic or with ribs, that goes from waist to breast. Used in the nineteenth century to obtain a narrow-waisted line. It developed from the Renaissance bodice, which was made rigid by two lengths of linen glued together.

In 1947 the corset was used to create the narrow waist required by the "new look." Dolce & Gabbana have "dignified" this garment, turning it into an item to be worn on the outside and interpreting it in precious fabrics, from satin to lace to hand-painted wool.

CORSET-COVER. A small undershirt to cover a corset. Originally from the nineteenth century, it is used today by Dolce & Gabbana as an alternative to a vest. Made from patchwork since the early 1990s, or from floral prints or fabrics with chinoiserie embroidery, they are an integral part of the Dolce & Gabbana style and are often worn under men's jackets.

CORSET-GIRDLE. A high girdle of elastic fabric which replaces the bodice in women's clothing. Figuratively, women's clothing that emphasizes the lines of the body.

A real item of clothing in the Dolce & Gabbana collections, it has gone from being an undergarment to an outer garment. It can be made of brocades, lace, velvet, tulle, satin, silk, cloth, nylon.

CROCHET. An artisan lace made by weaving threads of various dimensions with a special hooked needle (crochet-hook) to create small pieces that are then put together to form a larger design. Evoking the shawls of women of the South, the designers have created dresses, skirts, little sweaters, and overcoats. In addition, they are often embroidered, becoming even more precious.

CROSS. Historically an important motif for many ancient populations. In the west, it is the principal symbol of Christianity. A typical "jewel" to be worn from a thin chain around the neck. A common gift for various religious occasions. It has become part of the Dolce & Gabbana style and, sometimes embellished with diamonds, has been used in many of their collections.

EX VOTO. An object given in offering, following a solemn promise made to a divinity. A typical object found in chapels and churches. It can be made from any material. Connecting it to the culture of the South, where the ex voto shows the scene or situation from which one has been saved, Dolce & Gabbana have reproduced some of the most interesting ex voto, turning them into jewelry or using them on vests and handbags.

FILET. An artisan lace, a type of gridwork with various designs created with a darning stitch. Great lightness and transparency. Typical process used by the designers for shawls, dresses, and shirts.

KITSCH. Indicates products that exhibit false aesthetic values. With the crisis about the authenticity of the artistic product, the term tends to indicate a transgression within the aesthetic framework (for example: pop art's tendency to reify). In this spirit, the designers introduce kitsch elements into their collections, but only as a desire to shatter the bourgeois canons of elegance.

THE LEOPARD. Director: Luchino Visconti.

Actors: Burt Lancaster, Alain Delon, Claudia Cardinale.

Plot: Set in Sicily which is in tumult because of the arrival of Garibaldi's troops. Prince don Fabrizio di Salina (Lancaster) senses the changing times and allows his nephew Tancredi (Delon) to enlist as a volunteer and to become engaged to a beautiful young woman (Cardinale)—wealthy, but not from the nobility. Perhaps Visconti's most popular film, it is a faithful and opulent illustration of Sicily's transition from the Bourbons to the House of Savoy.

Costumes: Piero Tosi. The garments are a marvelous historical reconstruction of the era. Dolce & Gabbana were inspired by Don Fabrizio's impeccable hunting outfits in thick, costly velvets; vests; overcoats; and elegant smoking jackets. The unforgettable Claudia Cardinale, in the final dance sequence, with her white dress that shows off all her beauty, has been a key personality in the young designers' imaginations.

LIBERTY (ART NOUVEAU) CORSELET. Female undergarment, introduced at the beginning of the twentieth century. This was a corset with buttoned fastenings down the front, made up of a series of soft, knitted, fabric bands, sewn together with ribbons. The designers have reinterpreted this garment in various materials and have transformed it into a vest, or little shirt, thereby distancing it from its original use.

MAGNANI. Anna Magnani made her film debut in 1935. She played the lower class Pina, in *Rome, Open City* (1945) by Roberto Rossellini, where she revealed her extraordinary dramatic talents.

Portraying a woman of the people—strong, generous, sincere to the point of insolence—in other films of varying importance, she became a key figure in the rebirth of Italian postwar cinema. One of the greatest Italian actresses, she was also a woman who dictated a very specific style. Dresses with aprons; shirt-waist dresses, always a bit unbuttoned at the breast; little laced-up sweaters with the bra showing; undershirts; sandals with heels; narrow skirts with clinging shirts, always a bit unbuttoned; large overcoats, worn without stockings; the inevitable little black bag; and twin-sets. Simultaneously sexy and strong, she has been an extremely significant figure in the designers' imagination. Their women are always related to a Magnani ideal. Dark, shapely, feminine—she personifies the stereotype of the woman of the South. The "authentic" way of dressing, utilized in all neorealist cinema, is another point of reference in Dolce and Gabbana's culture, but they always succeed in making it real, never quoting it too literally.

PASOLINI. Pier Paolo Pasolini: writer, essayist, director. He made his debut with *Accattone,* the first in a series of films set in the working class world of Rome. He presented a different, non-conformist voice and was able to denounce the violence of social structures in the industrialized nations and his nostalgia for the values of the rural world. His characters are true symbols of an era and a way of life in their type of beauty, their way of dressing, and their attitude. Dolce & Gabbana have been fascinated by this director and have translated his images into modern terms.

PATCHWORK. A motif obtained by sewing together pieces of fabric that differ from each other in quality or color. Fashionable in the early 1970s, it was adopted by the designers throughout their line. They have used printed brocade, wool, velvet, tweed and even printed chiffon. Mixing together these materials, they have created overcoats, vests, dresses, trousers, and shirts, as well as carpets, footstools, armchairs, curtains, and other items for the home. They have also used leather or spotted fur combined with other fabrics to create accessories such as shoes and handbags as well as clothing.

PEASANT CAP. Black velvet with a visor, typical of field-watchers (the custodians of Sicilian estates), later a symbol of the Sicilian man, even if, in reality, it is now exclusively a literary reference.

As an object of fashion, it was first seen on the women's runway in 1986, at the Dolce & Gabbana fashion show, used to accentuate the "Mafioso" air of the man-styled suits in velvet, worn with vests and white shirts. It became an identifiable sign of their style. In addition to velvet and fustian (a coarse twill), which were the original materials used for the cap, patchwork, animal prints, and other cloths and prints have also been utilized. Today the cap is used equally in the women's and men's collections.

PETTICOAT. An under-skirt. In the Middle Ages this was a female undergarment similar to a quilted vest. When it was replaced by a shirt, it became an underskirt, fastened at the waist with ribbons or strings. Dolce and Gabbana were inspired by a certain type of petticoat that was quite fashionable in the late nineteenth century, with cords for lifting the skirts to facilitate navigating the streets. It became a Dolce & Gabbana classic and was used for several seasons, developing into fantastic, ample, "changeable" skirts.

PUPPET THEATER. Marionette performances of medieval epics (also recurrent in the famous primitive style paintings that adorn the carts drawn by donkeys), which express, in folk terms, an ethical ideal. The criminal degeneration of this courtly ideal exists or rather, existed, in the Mafia. Their expressive and contrasting use of colors has inspired the designers' use of color.

Sciascia. Leonardo Sciascia, wrote tales that are essays at heart. Many island points of reference, clothed in narrative form. His Sicilian nature has always been very strong, and his magical and evocative expressions of that world have entered the common vocabulary. His stories reveal a main source for the designers' inspiration, and, indeed, Sciascia's women seem to come alive on the Dolce & Gabbana runway.

Shawls. A typical element of the Dolce & Gabbana look. Beginning with their very first collection, the shawl has been interpreted in various ways: printed in vivid colors, embroidered, or done in simple black wool or silk. Always with long fringe.

"That some working class women still wear black shawls up to their eyes is not sufficient reason to identify considerable Islamic vestiges in the spiritual dress of Sicily." (Giuseppe Antonio Borgese)

Sicilian Cart. A small, two-wheeled cart for transporting goods, the sides decorated with characteristic colored designs, pulled by a gaudily bridled horse.

An inspirational motif for embroideries and prints, it reflects Sicilian culture, its sunny atmosphere, and its strong colors. Used as an inspirational motif at the beginning of their career, it has never been abandoned. Present in their winter 1998 collection, it is used in the printed fabric for shawls and coupled with heavy tweeds.

Sicilian Embroidery. Designed on muslin or percale with herring-bone-stitch embroidery or with embroidery that forms motifs similar to eyelet, to give the appearance of lace.

Sicily. "The Sicilian landscape. A landscape of vitality and sweetness, as if nature gave birth to it and art has composed and recomposed it. One needs to swoop down onto the island and embrace it in a single glance, in the entire prism of its colors: the brown of the mountains, the iron-gray of the volcanic magma, the wine color of the sea, the yellow of the sand, the insolent blue of the sky, the dark green of the chestnut trees, the silver green of the olives." (Gesualdo Bufalino)

A portrait of the Sicilian man or woman: "Pride as well as baronial haughtiness; jealousy, forces of love and hatred; the endurance of fidelity and vendetta; loyalty even when involving evil; generosity, if generosity can exist, even in crime—these are proverbial traits." (Giuseppe Antonio Borgese)

All these colors, these images, these visions are part of a history that has made suggestions to Dolce & Gabbana and continues to stimulate their imagination.

STAYS. A light girdle in elastic, or with elastic side panels, without stays, introduced in the 1920s. It covers the stomach and hips and supports the stockings with garters. The entire image of the women of the South is tied to this defining element of Dolce & Gabbana style. Almost exclusively black, attached to black stockings, opaque or transparent with seams. It is the most quoted feature of the Dolce & Gabbana woman. In its most recent evolution the stockings are embroidered with "Chinese" designs and the corsets are made of fabrics that are particularly precious, such as damasks; or they are made from extremely high-tech materials, such as reflective plastics. Red is offered as an alternative to black.

STAYS WITH TIES. Originally shaped by two pieces of rigid fabric, one in front, one in back, this garment dates back to the seventeenth century. It was made out of heavy linen or cotton, stiffened with whale bones, cane, or metal, and fastened in the back. During the second half of the nineteenth century, the term "corset" began to be used instead of "stays."

For the designers, the emphasis of the female body, creating new proportions, is fundamental. The corset, in its most varied uses, is a point of departure for the line of their clothes.

TANK TOP. A light undershirt of wool or cotton, very low-cut and sleeveless, similar to the undershirt used by oarsmen. Introduced in the early nineteenth century, with short shoulder-pads and extending to the waist, based on the model of the soft corselet or sleeveless shirt. It was originally worn as a protective layer between the corset and the dress; at the beginning of the twentieth century, when many women were refusing to wear corsets, it was worn directly in contact with the skin. Originally made from cotton or batiste, the most elegant versions were decorated with lace, while satin and silk were in vogue during the 1930s. For men, it was a garment to be worn under the shirt. Italian neorealist films identified this garment with young toughs, working-class men, or peasants. Used by the designers in combination with pin-striped trousers or under tailored double-breasted suits, it has been equally used for women's clothing. It is the absolute symbol of Dolce & Gabbana's "male" style. Today it is made in white or black ribbed cotton, with the logo on the outside.

VEST. A type of men's garment, without sleeves, worn beneath a jacket. With a long tradition as a sign of refinement and elegance, it has been created in silk fabrics and richly decorated. Only later was it combined with jackets and then made in the same fabric. In the late 1960s it was introduced into women's wardrobes as an expression of the prevailing unisex fashion. A key item in the very early Dolce & Gabbana collections, it defined a male-female ambiguity. The vest has undergone continuous development, both in shape and in fabrics.

VELVET. A typical fabric, with a soft, raised surface: it can be made of silk, cotton, wool, velvet, or corduroy and has been used by the designers for jackets, trousers, collars, and lapels of velvet. From the Latin *vellus*, "fleece" or "tufted pile." It is a tightly woven fabric with a short and dense pile that gives the surface a precious and soft appearance. From the famous winter 1988/1989 collection, inspired by *The Leopard* (see *Leopard*), velvet has always been present in the designers' collections for both sporty and elegant apparel, including vests and shoes. It was later embroidered, cut up to create patchwork motifs, and printed with both floral and animal-spot designs.

VISCONTI. A world-famous director, he represented a decadent and shadowy aesthetic, inspired by the literature of Dostoevsky, Camus, and Mann and by the music of composers such as Wagner and Verdi.

His career began with the neorealist film *Obsession*, and it is precisely this vein that is closest to the designers' sensibility. Visconti loved the use of black and white and the culture of the South. Inspired by the Sicily of Verga's *Malavoglia*, he made *The Earth Trembles*; he created a neorealist masterpiece with *Bellissima*, starring Magnani; and there is always *Rocco and His Brothers*, from that same period. With *The Leopard*, he returned to the Sicilian land (see *The Leopard*). Visconti's sets and his portrayal of nature as well as his costumes (see the tank top in *Rocco and His Brothers*) and frame of mind are an integral part of Dolce & Gabbana's imagination.

VOILE, or veil; noun. A very fine, light, transparent fabric; it can be loosely woven, dense or folded; a voile scarf; a voile dress; a head-cover, put on before entering church. "Above the white veil circle of olives, Woman appeared to me."(Dante) Sometimes, more generically, a fabric of various types, functioning as a cover.

A typical Dolce & Gabbana piece, indispensable for a Sicilian woman's every-day use, a manifestation of timidity and cleanliness. It has been interpreted in various ways by the designers, both in ways it can be worn and in the use of materials. The maximum expression of female sensuality, the veil becomes a play of seduction.

SICILIA

CHRONOLOGY

1958 : Domenico Dolce born in Polizzi Generosa (Palermo) on August 13

1962 : Stefano Gabbana born in Milan on November 14

1982 : Domenico Dolce and Stefano Gabbana opened their first studio

1985 : October: First appearance of the Dolce & Gabbana brand name at the Milano Collezioni fashion show in the New Talents category

1986 : March: First self-produced collection and fashion show, "Real Woman"

1987 : March: First women's knitwear collection

August: Opened new showroom at Via Santa Cecilia, 7, Milan

1988 : October: Ready-to-wear production agreement with Dolce Saverio, clothing firm owned by Domenico Dolce's family, based in Legnano (near Milan)

1989 : April: First women's fashion show in Tokyo

July: First lingerie and beachwear collections

1990 : January: First men's collection

April: First combined men's and women's fashion show in New York

October: Trade agreement with the Genny Group of Ancona as fashion consultants for the Complice line (ends in 1994)

November: Opened showroom in New York, 532 Broadway

1991 : June: Received Woolmark Award for most innovative men's collection of the year

September: First women's scarf collection on license

1992 : January: First men's tie collection on license

July: First men's beachwear collection on license

October: Bridal collection introduced
First women's perfume produced and distributed by Euroitalia,
Dolce & Gabbana Parfum

1993 : January: First men's underwear collection on license

May: Opened new men's and women's showroom at Piazza Umanitaria, 2, Milan
Dolce & Gabbana Parfum awarded international prize of the Perfume Academy as best female fragrance of the year

1994 : January: New young people's collection, "D&G Dolce & Gabbana," produced and distributed throughout the world by Ittierre of Isernia.
Presentation of first men's collection

February: Opened Dolce & Gabbana boutique in Milan, Via della Spiga, 2: men's and women's prêt-à-porter

March: Presented first women's collection: "D&G Dolce & Gabbana"

April: Introduced bath range, "Dolce & Gabbana Ligne de Bain"

Spring/Summer Collection 1988. Model: Marpessa.
© Photo: Ferdinando Scianna

June: Opened Dolce & Gabbana Home Collection shop at Via della Spiga, 2, Milan: carpets, cushions, footstools, handpainted ceramics

November: Men's perfume, *Dolce & Gabbana pour Homme*, produced and distributed by Euroitalia

1995 : January: Opened D&G shop at Corso Venezia, 7, Milan: clothes, jeans, accessories for men and women
"Dolce & Gabbana Jeans" collection introduced for men and women

April: *Dolce & Gabbana Pour Homme* received the international prize from the Academy of Perfume for best masculine fragrance, best packaging, and best campaign of the year.

September: Opened a new design studio in Milan (Via San Damiano, 7)

December: Dolce & Gabbana signed a contract with Marcolin for the launch of a collection of men's and women's eyewear.

1996 : March: On the occasion of their tenth anniversary, published the book, 10 Years of Dolce & Gabbana, an anthology of the most significant advertising images and editorials by the designers (Italian edition published by Leonardo Arte, English edition by Abbeville Press, German edition by Schirmer/Mosel Verlag)

April: Distribution contract with the Japanese group Misaki Shoji for the "Dolce & Gabbana" and "D&G" lines in Japan, and the opening of boutiques

May: For the first time, the French "Oscar des Parfums" award is given to an Italian fragrence, *Dolce & Gabbana Pour Homme*

May: Launched the bath range, "Dolce & Gabbana for Men"

June: Released a CD single entitled "D&G Music"

September: Dolce & Gabbana named Best Designer of the Year by the readers of the British magazine *FHM*

November: The first fashion show in New York for the "D&G" young line (Spring/Summer collection, 1997)

1997 : April: Inauguration of the new factory, Dolce Saverio S.p.A. in Legnano, which produces the Dolce & Gabbana ready-to-wear lines for men and women. The buildings, designed by the architect Gian Maria Torno, occupied an area of 120,000 square meters.

June: Released the CD single, "D&G More More More"

September: Opened Dolce & Gabbana Boutique in New York, 825 Madison Avenue
Opened D&G boutique in New York, 434 West Broadway, Soho

October: For second year running, Dolce & Gabbana acclaimed Best Designer of the Year by readers of British magazine *FHM*

November: New fragrance for men and women, *By Dolce & Gabbana*, introduced

December: Dolce & Gabbana named footwear designer of the year by American magazine *Footwear News*
Dolce & Gabbana Wildness is published, a collection of the most significant editorial images based on the animal-print motif

1998 : January: Opened women's accessories boutique at Corso Venezia, 12, Milan

March: Opened new New York showroom, 660 Madison Avenue

May: Launched D&G eyewear collection

Spring/Summer Collection 1992. Model: Monica Bellucci.
© Photo: Steven Meisel.

Dolce & Gabbana

L'Isola dei Siciliani, photo taken from the book by Diego Mormorio and Giuseppe Leone (Peliti Associati Editore). © Photo: Giuseppe Leone.

Spring/Summer Collection 1988. Model: Marpessa. © Photo: Ferdinando Scianna.
Spring/Summer Collection 1989. Model: Maria Cabrera. © Photo: Gianpaolo Barbieri.

Spring/Summer Collection 1994. © Photo: Mario Sorrenti.
Spring/Summer Collection 1988. Model: Marpessa. © Photo: Ferdinando Scianna.

Les Siciliens, photo taken from the book by Dominique Fernandez and Leonardo Sciascia published by éditions Denoël. © Photo: Ferdinando Scianna.

Fall/Winter Collection 1987–1988. © Photo: Ferdinando Scianna.
Spring/Summer Collection 1994. Model: Nina Brosh. © Photo: Mario Sorrenti.

Sicilia Ritrovata, photo taken from the book by Antonino Buttitta and Melo Minnella (Cavallotto Editore, Catania). © Photo: Melo Minnella.
Photo appearing in British *Elle* (February 1994). Models: Kate Moss and Emma Balfour. © Photo: Thierry Le Goues/Elle/Scoop.

Photo appearing in *Harper's Bazaar Uomo* (September–October 1990).
© Photo Stefano Beggiato.
Spring/Summer Collection 1989. Model: Cristina Cascardo. © Photo: Gianpaolo Barbieri.

Il Barocco in Sicilia, photo taken from the book by Vincenzo Consolo and Giuseppe Leone (Bompiani Editore). © Photo: Giuseppe Leone.
Fall/Winter Collection 1997–1998. Model: Danielle Zinaich. © Photo: Steven Meisel.

Spring/Summer Collection 1987. Model: Amira Casar. © Photo: Fabrizio Ferri.

Spring/Summer Collection 1996. Model: Linda Evangelista. © Photo: Steven Meisel.
Fall Winter Collection 1989–1990. Model: Isabella Rossellini. © Photo: Steven Meisel.

Fall/Winter Collection 1996–1997. Model: Elsa Benitez. © Photo: Steven Meisel.
Fall/Winter Collection 1996–1997. Models: Elsa Benitez and Enrique Palacios. © Photo: Steven Meisel.

Fall/WinterCollection 1990–1991. Model: Tony Ward. © Photo: Steven Meisel.
Fall/Winter Collection 1996–1997. Model: Elsa Benitez. © Photo: Steven Meisel.

Photo appearing in Italian *Vogue* (March 1989). Models: Linda Evangelista and Cindy Crawford. © Photo: Peter Lindbergh.
Sicilia Ritrovata, photo taken from the book by Antonino Buttitta and Melo Minnella (Cavallotto Editore, Catania). © Photo: Melo Minnella.

Fall/Winter Collection 1994–1995. Model: Isabella Rossellini. © Photo: Michel Comte.
Spring/Summer Collection 1996. Model: Tony Ward. © Photo: Steven Meisel.

Spring/Summer Collection 1995. Model: Isabella Rossellini. © Photo: Michel Comte.
Sicilia Ritrovata, photo taken from the book by Antonino Buttitta and Melo Minnella (Cavallotto Editore, Catania). © Photo: Melo Minnella.

Fall/Winter Collection 1992–1993. Models: Nadja Auermann, Meghan Douglas and Angelika Kallio. © Photo: Steven Meisel.
Photo appearing in Italian *Vogue* (February 1991). Models: Linda Evangelista, Naomi Campbell and Christy Turlington. © Photo: Peter Lindbergh.

Photo appearing in L'*Uomo Vogue* (November 1991). © Photo: Giovanni Gastel.
Fall/Winter Collection 1994–1995. Model: Isabella Rossellini. © Photo: Michel Comte.

Photo appearing in Italian *Vogue* (October 1994). Model: Felicitas Kohl. © Photo: Helmut Newton.
Fall/WinterCollection 1991–1992. Model: Sherilyn Fenn. © Photo: Steven Meisel.

Spring/Summer Collection 1990. Model: Veruschka. © Photo: Steven Meisel.
Fall/Winter Collection 1990–1991. Models: Christy Turlington and Tony Ward. © Photo: Steven Meisel.

Fall/Winter Collection 1995–1996. Model: Linda Evangelista. © Photo: Steven Meisel.
Fall/Winter Collection 1995–1996. Model: Eric Yetter. © Photo: Steven Meisel.

Fall/Winter Collection 1993–1994. Model: Justin Chambers. © Photo: Mario Sorrenti.
Fall/Winter Collection 1993–1994. Models: Michele Hicks and Natane Adcock. © Photo: Steven Meisel.

Fall/Winter Collection 1994–1995. Model: Isabella Rossellini. © Photo: Michel Comte.
Fall/Winter Collection 1994–1995. Model: Isabella Rossellini. © Photo: Michel Comte.

Fall/Winter Collection 1994–1995. Model: Isabella Rossellini. © Photo: Michel Comte.
Spring/Summer Collection 1995. Domenico Dolce and Stefano Gabbana model their own creations. © Photo: Michel Comte.

The publisher would like to thank the house of Dolce & Gabbana, and most particularly Carla Buzzi and Anja Köhne for their assistance in producing this book.

Equal thanks to Ruven Afanador, Gianpaolo Barbieri, Stefano Beggiato, Michel Comte, Fabrizio Ferri, Giovanni Gastel, Thierry Le Goues, Giuseppe Leone, Peter Lindbergh, Melo Minnella, Helmut Newton, Ferdinando Scianna and Mario Sorrenti, and especially to Steven Meisel.

In addition, thanks to Natane Adcock, Monica Bellucci, Marpessa Hennink, Amira Casar, Christy Turlington, Naomi Campbell, Kate Moss, Veruschka, Cindy Crawford, Nadja Auermann, Emma Balfour, Elsa Benitez, Nina Brosh, Cristina Cascardo, Justin Chambers, Meghan Douglas, Sherilyn Fenn, Michele Hicks, Angelica Kallio, Felicitas Kohl, Enrique Palacios, Tony Ward, Maria Cabrera, Eric Yetter, Danielle Zinaich, and most particularly to Linda Evangelista and Isabella Rossellini.

Finally, this book would not have been possible without the generous contribution of Jim Moffat (president of Art & Commerce), Caren Clarke and Rosanna Sguerra (Art & Commerce), Marie-Christine Biebuyck (Magnum), David and Alex (Elite), Susanne Moninger (German *Vogue*), Jed Root (Corinne Karr), Marina Rossi (Italian *Vogue*), Sandrine and Hélène (Filomeno), Jeff Sowards (Michel Comte), Sylviane (*Elle*/Scoop), and Barbara Tubaro (TDR).